X

Winner of the
2023 Wil Mills Award
West Chester University Poetry Center

FOSSIL
&
WING

JASON BARRY

DOS MADRES

2023

DOS MADRES PRESS INC.

P.O. Box 294, Loveland, Ohio 45140
www.dosmadres.com   editor@dosmadres.com

Dos Madres is dedicated to the belief that the small press is essential to the vitality of contemporary literature as a carrier of the new voice, as well as the older, sometimes forgotten voices of the past. And in an ever more virtual world, to the creation of fine books pleasing to the eye and hand.

Dos Madres is named in honor of Vera Murphy and Libbie Hughes, the "Dos Madres" whose contributions have made this press possible.

Dos Madres Press, Inc. is an Ohio Not For Profit Corporation and a 501 (c) (3) qualified public charity. Contributions are tax deductible.

Executive Editor: Robert J. Murphy

Illustration & Book Design: Elizabeth H. Murphy
www.illusionstudios.net

Typeset in Adobe Garamond Pro & EngraversMT
ISBN 978-1-953252-92-0
Library of Congress Control Number: 2023944371

First Edition

ACKNOWLEDGEMENTS

Poems in this collection have appeared in journals, to whose editors grateful acknowledgement is made.

236 Journal: "Among the Weka"
32 Poems: "Fishing"
Angle: "Driftwood," "In Poland," "Intuition"
Bad Lilies: "Mid-Autumn"
Cimarron Review: "Pruning"
Citron Review: "Buntings"
Cortland Review: "Hibiscus," "Slate"
Crab Creek Review: "Just the two of us, this once," "Tracks"
Poet Lore: "Mannequin"
Poetry Ireland Review: "Dear John"
Raintown Review: "Together Still"
Thrush Poetry Journal: "Metro-North"

Special thanks to Annie Finch, Bob Hildreth, Ada Limón, the Iris N. Spencer Foundation, the West Chester University Poetry Center and Poetry by the Sea, and to my classmates and teachers at Boston University's MFA Program in Creative Writing. Additionally, I am grateful for the artistic and intellectual friendship I've shared over the years with Roy Bentley, Dean Birkenkamp, Charles Doersch, Aaron Leroux, D. Eric Parkison, and Eric Westerlind. Finally, I thank my whole family and especially my wife, Lydia Barry, for their loving support.

for Eric Westerlind

CONTENTS

I.

II.

III.

FOSSIL
&
WING

I

METRO-NORTH

Glenwood, Irvington, Scarborough, Poughkeepsie.
Weeds on the track,

A hot, hot track.
Up ahead, a kingbird toes the line,

A bald conductor dives into his plum.
Then, with the gas, a lurch—

Wings start to thrash,
Currents in a deep sea of sky.

Dolphin cloud. Coral cloud.
Octopus and crab.

This pressed spirit,
Clawing its way out of the shell.

BUNTINGS

Father told me once to
be a man

for I was not meant to sketch
a daffodil   or chase the buntings

as they swooped like paper planes
from our red chimney

flight lines of curlicues and
feathers

don't just sit there
he'd say on Sunday mornings

fishing rods in hand
but I'd grin and let my feet

dangle down into the water
toes tickled by the skins

of passing trout
when I was eight years old

I learned what all sons know
Uncle Rick's daughter in our garage

if you mention this to anyone
I'll destroy you   Dad said

grey hands like shattered clay on
a child's breast

we walked into the study
that autumn evening

sunset painted above the lake
I remember him whispering that

these suckers pack a heavy punch
twenty hollow-points in a plastic box

pro-casing
heart-crushing
silver-feeling

he placed a shell in my jacket pocket
kissed my forehead lightly

and said to play in the field
out back with Jenny

TOGETHER STILL

Imagine now that we could still be friends,
that I could take back everything I said,
the awkward gesture, the mistimed amends,
that I'd been cautious when I went ahead.
We'd meet on weekends, take the kids to walk
along the river, enjoy the breeze and view.
(Our wives would lag behind so they could talk).
I'd try to keep myself from watching you,
your torso lovely, the way you would stand
beside the water when we were away.
I'd tell myself to not reach for your hand
or say the things I said that other day.
The lives we now have would not then exist
if I had stopped when you tried to resist.

MID-AUTUMN

When you left,
my place became
disheveled: a sluff of clothes
beside dirty sheets,

the window sills
blanketed with dust,
my golden ficus slumped
over the sink. Desire

failed. August light
turned to brittle husk.
It's been over
a month since you've been gone.

After my showers now—
the bathroom window
cracked for cool air—
I leave warm

droplets on my skin,
the steam-stick
on the mirror. Another
person comes to wipe it off.

SLATE

Perhaps this is the way it ought to be,
The coastal light is tame and beautiful.
A wave of silence spreads across the sea
Beneath the two-tone plumage of a gull.

If what we are is bone and memory,
And sensory is synonym for soul—
I wonder what will then become of me,
When slate-white feathers wash up in the lull.

When slate-white feathers wash up in the lull,
I wonder what will then become of me.
Is sensory a synonym for soul,
If what we are is bone and memory?

Beneath the two-tone plumage of a gull,
A wave of silence spreads across the sea.
The coastal light is tame and beautiful,
Perhaps this is the way it ought to be.

DRIFTWOOD

for Skip

A black-backed gull
looks crosswise

at the sea, scans
the fading distance.

A tiger snail
leaves her imprint

on the sand. We, too,
are becoming old.

Yet I try to learn
the nature of driftwood,

the iodine way
of seagulls—

how silt
can make a fossil

of the wing.
Dearest,

does a year still add
another ring?

A stingray kite lines out
above the coast

and is summoned
again swiftly.

Night unfurls
between the dunes.

II

PRUNING

What stays in focus is the sound: the snap
of furrowed canes along the wire,
a crush of brittle leaves beneath the stride
and how, at certain times, the wind would
shape the fumes into a fox behind our truck.

Late June. An antipodal winter setting in,
the snip and wrap of cultivated vines.
One day the four of us at work—me and
three Brazilians—our steel shears snug
against the bark. That morning was as crisp

as ever: the distant mountains under snow
before the truck came, our drive through
the vineyards and a mist down in the valley.
Mute sky. A pair of stooping horses on
horizon, a dozen rows to go before the dark.

The afternoon was numb, and though his
features have gone frosty now, I see that old
Brazilian lop his thumb off by the pasture,
the flush of blood and half-congealed grime.
Wet hay. Another season's cut was underway.

DEAR JOHN

Forgive the cold formality
of this address, this letter that I've written
here in Boston, and which, I'm pretty sure—
before you even reach the final lines—
will re-ignite the feelings you've suppressed.
Please know I would have liked to talk about
these things, had you decided that we should.
But as it stands, this seems the only way
to start, to sweep the lies that have been told,
the ashes that have gathered over time.
All that you ever said is that he died
(a heart attack at fifty-six years old).
That was some time before you met Aileen,
before you had three kids and started at your firm.
I never really thought about him much,
or asked for you to tell me who he was.
And yet I think he must have been like you:
the way you grit your teeth when you get drunk,
your secrecy, your penchant for control.
Your siblings never once mentioned his name,
despite the years we met for holidays:
those dry Thanksgiving dinners at our house,
the Christmas mornings at your mother's place
in Cherry Creek, before the nursing home.
I used to meet for coffee with her there:
a claustrophobic room above the road,
the pewter light and crimson-velvet chairs.
She told me things that I already knew,
and asked me questions she'd already asked—
maybe you picked this habit up from her?

In any case, one day I helped her take
some things down from the shelf:
a Rolodex with names of former friends,
some unpaid bills and medical reports,
a box of photos taken in the war.
She showed me one of him, my grandfather:
a stern, good-looking guy, the stars and stripes
that draped over the engine of a plane—
the Captain's Ball in nineteen fifty-three.
We sipped our coffee. Shifted in our chairs.
I asked her then to tell me how he died.
His room was filled with books and copper pins,
with folded maps and fur-lined winter coats.
He shared a dorm with several other men,
a treatment center built after the war.
I see them smoking, legs crossed in their beds,
their suffocating boredom and withdrawal.
(Is this how you have also pictured it?)
The lights go down. A roof goes up in flames,
and through it all I see your father's face.
My teeth are clenched. My heart is beating fast.
As fast as it has ever beat before.
My bowels burn. The walls are melting now.
Before you put my letter on the desk
you should know I haven't told anyone else.
And if you want to talk, you know where you
can find me.

                    From your loving son—Jason

IN POLAND

That season was
a mild one, she says,
letting her pale lips
crack. But even so,
Europe's old lament
would not permit
the view of an evergreen.
Days and nights—
the ones she remembers
anyway—are void
along their edges,
though evening's
wine and song
have brought her gaze
centerfold.
She recalls a distant
wheat field, says
she can picture
the gift her father gave
before the light
scattered. The smell
of the evergreens.
She lifts her collar
higher now, asks
for brandy on the house.
The piano man puts down
another tune.

INTUITION

Phone call after phone call that autumn afternoon:
everyone said it was the worst damn thing.
And I said I'd felt it, knew she'd do it soon.
Phone call after phone call that autumn afternoon.
In the hospital's intensive care room,
I almost said it was a last blessing.
Phone call after phone call that autumn afternoon:
everyone said it was the worst damn thing.

TRACKS

after Alexander Scriabin

You took me to the edge of a sonic wood,
and I found it odorous, muculent, divine.

That was the year of infinite choice—
of new stars I mean, before shadowrise,

before the warm spindrift of desire
turned solid. Doubt silting deep in the mind.

Do I still hear it? Your touch fading now.
And yet, there are moments when

reflecting on that distance, glazed fresh or drawn
in rubato light, the bounds of what I love

or say I love, become something other.

MANNEQUIN

At no time has he fingered
legs as smooth, as perfectly
proportioned as these ones.
He starts out with the ankles,

strokes along the tendons
and then glides up toward
the buttocks. Cold knees.
He slides his hand between

the hamstrings, touching now
his member through the netting
of his shorts. Glass bulge.
He's never felt one like it,

has never touched another
but his own. It's at this moment
that a voice sounds in
the distance, his panicked

mother coming in a flash.
She yanks the boy's hand
from the swimsuit, says sorry
to the cashier when they go.

HIBISCUS

In the schoolyard
a girl cups a
spider
in her palm
the birthday gift
from a friend
raising it toward her
cheek
as if preparing for a kiss
she works to contain
the giggles
when a bell
sounds near
as though it were
a shriek
(an alarm)
she drops the
spider
on her
shoulder
like a penny
(or a parrot)
and I watch as it
glides along
her neck
chin
the lower lip
a breath
and it will dance

through the
hibiscus
delicate
symphony
eight feathery
legs
like magic
in the grasses

NEST

Each day when I go out
I see them there:
the strewn feathers

of a breast or wing,
the sun-dried needles,
a strand of hair or string.

They always build it
in that very spot
under the awning,

hidden by the shade
and crumpled fabric,
as if they won't be

caught, their efforts
not unmade.

AMONG THE WEKA

Stevensons Island, New Zealand

See again
the way the birds moved in,
their ducking under Mother—
seeking cover from

a shag or gull or whatever
it was that cast its
shadow onto landscape,
the fledging rails

finding solace under wing—
a rotting weasel carcass
between them and me.
Yet how they'd coo

and zee their necks as
soon as feeding moment
came, myself at first
intruder on the scene

and then—when birdseed
flew the air—how they'd
weave through tussock
grass near dock's landing.

Once I tossed grey
pellets by the handful
on the outcrop,
cocked my snare to

ready, and waited
for the foraging chicks
to tiptoe onto wire.
When they approached

the trap in pairs,
Mother's screech ricocheted
like a ring around
the island and they

scattered, headlong under
fern and feather canopy—
safe at least until
the rats came around.

DREAM CANYON

And here they stand now
three aging sisters
at the edge of the water
the last skiff trailing in to dock

they look back on their lives
the contour of this valley
the sandstone marked
by river grime

and they recollect now
how they drifted
through Dream Canyon
the silted light

splattered against the pine
high clouds pool
a piece of scree slides
tumbles toward the water

a mirror image breaks
across the surface
they are not themselves
any longer

they're an antler shed
furrowed on the shore
an angler's footprint
after summer rain

they're the hatching
mayflies in the shadows
the resin swelling
when the light drains

THE CROSSING

She knew that it would be by boat. That much
was certain. But whether it be made of oak
or iron, and if they'd be departing under

starlight, she wasn't sure. In recent nights,
her mind's eye had dreamt it such:
the curved bow engraved with silver flowers,

a dangling oar on both sides of the vessel.
Faint lamp. And who the captain of this ship
would be, that too was no more than a guess—

yes, perhaps someone she'd seen before,
but couldn't say from where. Blue eyes
brilliant, his dark beard fraying at the edges.

And would she be allowed to say goodbye,
she wondered? And would she be on time?
What if she were late! She pictures others there,

their clothes beside the water, their names
drying in the open ledger. They're asking
where she is, and where they will be going,

and if the river always flows this slowly,
and if, when the mist comes rolling through
the valley, they'll still be near the shoreline.

FISHING

in memory of Kim Bridgford

Only the birds with me at Derby Wharf,
The wind low, dawn's ripple
On the water's edge.
What is it I'm trying to say?

That since your passing,
Riven like a split shot,
The driftwood reeking in sand. . .
Words snag.

I make way slowly up the dock,
Cast another line.
A gull pushes off from its stone.
Nothing bites.

JUST THE TWO OF US, THIS ONCE

There isn't much
to graze on for a deer

at this late hour
no patch of grass

beneath the desert bluffs
wind-swept chimneys

pinyon-prickled sky
she stoops and sniffs

the ground a second time
calyx of golden yarrow

my fire gone to ember
gone to ash

the turn and glance
and one half-frozen eye

breath gives
a scattering of bone

beside the camp
tent-clap in the breeze

long way from the city
the bracing herd

About the Author

JASON BARRY holds an MFA from Boston University and is pursuing further studies at St Anne's College, University of Oxford. His poems have appeared in *Barrow Street, 32 Poems, The Cortland Review, Poetry Ireland Review, Crab Creek Review, Bad Lilies, Poet Lore, Thrush Poetry Journal, Cimarron Review,* and elsewhere. His work has been nominated for Best of the Net and other awards and his poetry was selected by Ada Limón to feature on *The Slowdown.* He has been offered artist scholarships and grants from Poetry by the Sea, Boston University, and the Massachusetts Cultural Council.

For the full Dos Madres Press catalog:
www.dosmadres.com